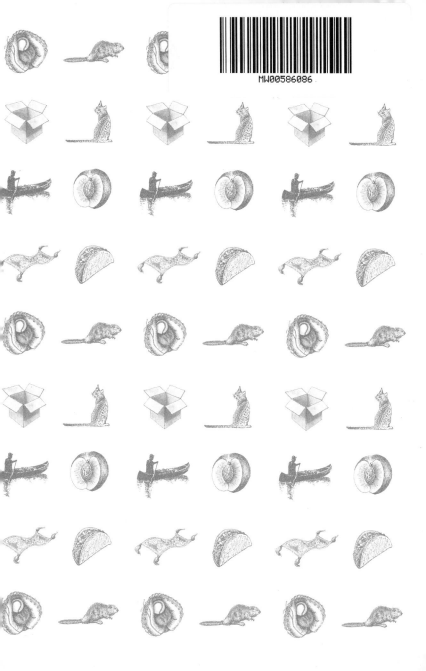

THE LESBIAN
SEX HAIKU BOOK
(with Cats!)

THE LESBIAN SEX HAIKU BOOK
(with Cats!)

ANNA PULLEY

Illustrations by Kelsey Beyer

FLATIRON
BOOKS
NEW YORK

THE LESBIAN SEX HAIKU BOOK (WITH CATS!).
Copyright © 2016 by Anna Pulley. Illustrations copyright
© 2016 by Kelsey Beyer. All rights reserved. Printed in China. For
information, address Flatiron Books, 175 Fifth
Avenue, New York, N.Y. 10010.

www.flatironbooks.com

Designed by Anna Gorovoy
Production Manager: Adriana Coada

The Library of Congress Cataloging-in-Publication Data
is available upon request.

ISBN 978-1-250-07264-1 (paper over board)
ISBN 978-1-250-07265-8 (e-book)

Our books may be purchased in bulk for promotional,
educational, or business use. Please contact your local bookseller or
the Macmillan Corporate and Premium Sales Department at
1-800-221-7945, extension 5442, or by e-mail at
MacmillanSpecialMarkets@macmillan.com.

First Edition: April 2016

10   9   8   7   6   5   4   3   2   1

To our parents. None of whom are lesbians (or cats) but are nevertheless delightful.

CONTENTS

INTRODUCTION

In 2010, the girl I planned to marry dumped me. I had proposed to her nine months earlier, on the Isle of Lesbos, in Skala Eresou, where Sappho was born, in case we're playing Who's the Gayest. She decided she wasn't into ladies as much as she originally had thought. (For the record, she's a lovely person, and we are good friends now, because part of the lesbian hex—which affects even those who aren't lifers—involves remaining friends with your exes forever.) At the time, though, I was shattered. My chest was a brick, and I could do little besides cry-hyperventilate. I fantasized about getting hit by cars—not fatally so, just some light maiming—so that my ex would have to come back and take care of me and then decide to grow old with me the way we originally had planned.

Also, my dad had been recently diagnosed with lung cancer, and my stepdad had a stroke, and my mom ended up being hospitalized as well due to the stress of it all.

I had just started a new job ("paid internship" is a more accurate description) making about six dollars an hour in the most expensive city in the United States, a city I most certainly could not afford to live in on my own. It was not the greatest time to be dumped by my fiancée, as far as those things go.

And because of all these events, I couldn't write. I couldn't even journal. I peered at the stories of my life thus far and didn't recognize myself in any of them—they were like those dreams in which you wake up and remember nothing but the feeling they inspired. When I tried, my words would devolve into self-loathing expletives, like a fifth grader's reenactment of a Martin Scorsese movie. But I was also contractually obligated to write for work. And by "write," I mean tweet. So I did that, not just so I wouldn't get fired but also because it was strangely satisfying and required very little time commitment. Plus, it helped me avoid thinking about the emotional tsunami of suck that had become my life. A tweet, 140 characters. A haiku, seventeen syllables. A task that small and manageable I could do. Anyone can write seventeen syllables, I told myself. And so I did. I wrote one every day for a year, just like how Ryan Gosling's character wrote one letter every day for a year in *The Notebook*, because he was copying me. One of the first ones was this:

Being on Twitter
all day for work makes it hard
to finish any

And another:

I face all my fears
in yoga: flying, falling,
farting in public.

And another, and another. I wrote haiku until I no longer felt like I would die from ineptitude, or that my life was a huge cosmic mistake, particularly my hair and the errant incisor that made me appear to be always on the verge of toothing something. Not to get too Oprah one-thing-I-know-for-sure on you, but writing haiku was how I slowly re-raveled myself. I put my life back together three lines at a time.

My healing process was aided by two things: (1) a handful of beautiful, unavailable women and (2) an unwavering belief that poetry would make those women want to have sex with me. Of course this strategy failed a lot of times. (How often? It's not like I counted. Fourteen.) But it also worked a great many times too. It led to a four-year sexy-romance-heart-tumble-thing with a married woman who lived on the other side of the country. We wrote a lot of haiku to each other. Hundreds of them. It also led to a one-night stand with a straight girl I met on Twitter. It led to two fuck buddies developing feelings for each other and ceasing to fuck me (see Chapter 5, "How Lesbian Sex Works"). It led me to bars (see Chapter 2, "How to Pick Up a Lesbian") and sex parties and sex dungeons and spectacular rejections and spectacular hangovers and some truly amazing friendships (see Chapter 8, "My Ex Is Your Ex"), and eventually it led to a fantastic girlfriend who did not balk at all when I suggested we do a book together whereby she would draw cats in various states of lesbian anxiety (see Chapter 4, "U-Hauling").

WHAT'S A HAIKU, ANYWAY?

Our attention spans are getting shorter. Blame ADHD or the Internet if you must, but the truth of the matter is not much can hold our attention for long, even when it's about topics dear to our hearts, such as love, Nutella, or cunnilingus. This is why haiku was invented—to give our short-form brains something else to do when we aren't photographing dogs wearing leggings. The word "haiku" has been around since the nineteenth century, but it has appeared in other variations since as far back as the ninth century, when people had to actually memorize things in order to impress anyone.

What is a haiku, you ask? It's a form of poetry that the Japanese invented and that we Westerners graciously stole from them and changed ever so slightly to fit our language wonkiness. We mostly think of haiku as seventeen-syllable poems, in the 5-7-5 format, that look like this:

> I like poetry,
> flowers, and waterfalls. I'm
> a haiku genius!

Japanese haiku isn't based on syllables, however. It's based on *onji*, which are units of sound that don't correlate with English very well. The Haiku Society of America (which is a thing that exists!) explains, in a somewhat exasperated manner, that haiku isn't a type of fixed form poetry (like a sonnet, for instance) and that people should just get over the rigid 5-7-5 format already, because they were probably tired, as I was, of getting into Twitter fights with people over syllables. That said, I tried to adhere to this format when I could in this book because it's what most of us think of when we think of haiku, and because, like most lesbians, I am a pleaser.

In the West, haiku was popularized in the 1960s by writers like Jack Kerouac and Gary Snyder, though the trend was soon superseded by enthusiasm for hipsters, zombies, and vampires, per our collective cultural boner for brainless dead things that sparkle and drink PBR.

WHAT'S A LESBIAN, ANYWAY?

Like haiku and poetry in general, lesbians (and bisexuals, trans folk, queers, genderqueers, tenderqueers, hetero-flexibles, and all womyn-loving wimmin) are frequently misunderstood. Sure, you may have read about them once in a Women's Studies class, glimpsed them on *Grey's Anatomy* or in the plaster aisle at Home Depot, but it's a rare thing indeed to experience queer women in the wild. Who are these mythical beings? What do they do? What do they wear now that hipsters have appropriated flannel? How do they meet? Is it true that lesbians move in together after the second date? Is there a "man" in such relationships? And if so, can it be me? What does Rachel Maddow have that I don't? These are some of the questions you may have. This book aims to dispel myths, to enlighten, to demystify, to remystify, to gently chide, and to perplex your parents, all in the most straightforward medium available to humankind.

But first, a caveat! I am not out to speak for every queer lady. The following haiku are by no means trying to capture *the* lesbian experience, because there isn't one—it differs for every queer lady. I realize also that not every queer-identified person subscribes to female pronouns or female sex parts. I totally support that, but for ease and clarity, I decided to keep it simple. In fact, if you don't like a pronoun or genital reference, feel free to scratch it out and use whatever feels comfortable to you. I don't mind.

Careful observers might also notice that this is called *The Lesbian Sex Haiku Book*, but that it encompasses a lot more than that—breakups, makeups, friendship, courtship, etc. The reason that this is so is because sex is in a little bit of all we do. For a group that collectively eroticizes Teva sandals and Greenpeace, the sky is the limit, you know? It's also because maybe I secretly want confused heterosexual men to pick up this book and think it's porn and then be like, "Ahh, I just read lesbian poetry!" And join a coven in New Mexico. One can dream.

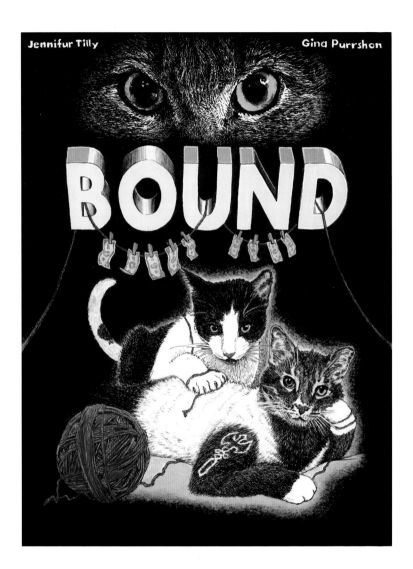

LESBIANISM 101

Have you always wondered if you might like girls *that way*, but weren't sure because you don't have several dietary restrictions and aren't perpetually covered in pet hair? If you don't know what a lesbian is but picked up this book because you are a cat who enjoys looking at pictures of other cats, then put it down, Mittens. This book is not string! If you are a human person who doesn't know what a lesbian is, but also doesn't know how to use the Internet or read a book or watch television or movies, then what do you do with yourself? I've always wondered.

Here's a haiku definition:

> Lesbianism:
> So much more than folk music
> and hemp shorteralls.

Now that that's cleared up, the following haiku present some indications that you might be, perhaps unbeknownst to you, sapphically inclined, bicurious, full-on lesbionic, or "in college."

YOU MIGHT BE A QUEER GIRL IF . . .

You can't even break
up with your therapist in
under a decade.

When an ex-lover
has thrown a Boca Burger
at you drunkenly.

When you live with your
ex far longer than you should
because "it's cheaper."

Do you own bongos?
A djembe? A didgeri-
don't-mind-if-you-do?

When asking, "What are
you thinking?" is your go-to
icebreaker question.

Does a "naked mud
dance" sound like a great way to
commune with nature?

Do you find yourself
wondering why songs don't have
more ukulele?

You are accused of
making uncomfortably
lengthy eye contact.

If you've gone out a
dozen times and still don't know
if you're dating her.

You obsessively
Google prospective dates in
the guise of "research."

You play flag football
but are, by every other
measure, an adult.

Do you own more than
one vest that your mother did
not purchase for you?

You have developed
unhealthy attachments to
several baristas.

The only "doctors"
you are familiar with are
Bronner and Martens.

When you dance, does it
look like you're Hula-Hooping
in a wild typhoon?

You're allergic to everything—except passive-aggressive memos.

You have at least four jobs at any given time, and you volunteer.

You've got 99 problems and 98 of them are your "bitches."

A REPRESENTATIVE SAMPLE OF EVERY LESBIAN MOVIE EVER MADE

Lesbian films serve many important functions—visibility, levity, fodder for processing, etc.—but their most important function is to make us feel better about staying alive so well because most lesbian and bisexual characters in contemporary queer films (and television) die horrible deaths. Ha-ha, weird, right? But seriously, congratulations on not dying. You are great at that. Hopefully.

Girl has sexual
awakening with teacher/
roommate/friend. Then dies.

Girl has horrible,
traumatic past, present, and
future. Then she dies.

Girl has sexual
awakening with druggie.
The drug addict dies.

Girl has sexual
awakening. Kills her mom/
lover for "funsies."

Girl has lesbian
tryst during the Holocaust.
Everybody dies.

Girl has sexual
awakening, decides she
likes men. She still dies.

Girl doesn't have a
sexual awakening,
but she shaves her head!

Cheerleader figures
out she's gay. NO ONE DIES! Film
revered forever.

Gina Gershon wears
a tight tank top. Sorry, does
something else happen?

First hour: eating.
Second hour: fucking. And
third hour: crying.

Straight-looking girl goes
gay. Male director slowly
jerks off for two hours.

Girl spends half the film
staring vacantly into
bodies of water.

Married lesbians
suffer from bed death, but can
still be great parents!

Hetero subplot
is added to make straights feel
okay with "gay stuff."

HOW TO PICK UP
A LESBIAN

Picking up a lesbian is not as easy as it looks, even though many are around five feet tall. For starters, it's difficult to tell simply from appearances what ladies walking among us might be receptive to seeing us naked. Unless your potential paramour is wearing a sign that says "My other ride is your face!" it's not often obvious that you are in fact courting a lady-lovin' lady. There are a few signifiers to look for, of course—short asymmetrical haircuts, Coexist T-shirts, a preponderance of jorts in her wardrobe—but nothing foolproof. Just ask the countless lesbians who have mistakenly ogled both the teenage boy *and* his heterosexual mother sporting a mullet and a college sweatshirt because they thought they were lesbians. Alas, until the day comes when we decide to help potential lovers decipher our sexual proclivities with, say, a large face tattoo, we can only surmise, ask questions, and take chances. That said, however, the following haiku provide a jumping-off point to picking up the gay gal of your dreams using well-worn approaches field-tested in places as diverse as bars, gender studies classes, and the modular cube aisle at the Container Store.

MORE REALISTIC WAYS TO "FLAG" AS A WOMYN-LOVING WO'MOON

Host a dinner where
you promise to serve harm-free
vegan macro bowls.

Do not brush off the
cat (or dog) hair you are most
surely covered in.

When girl remarks on
pets' hair, say names are Vita
and Virginia.

I was serious
about that "My other ride
is your face" button.

Find an excuse to
take out your wallet so she
can see it's empty.

Stand in a corner
and refuse to drink all but
low-calorie beer.

Stand in a corner
and incessantly sweep your
hair out of your eyes.

"Hi. I would like to
officially invite you
to join my coven."

Introduce yourself
using the words "witch," "poet,"
"grad school," or "co-op."

FOOLPROOF LESBIAN
PICKUP LINES

Of course I read *Cunt*.
Painting with menstrual blood
was transformative!

Girl, I would love to
help you move that modular
couch from IKEA.

Cold? Take my micro-
fleece vest. I only wear it
ironically.

Have you reconciled
your identity with race
and class privilege?

Don't label me—I'm
a non-het-identified
poly pagan witch.

It has been MANY
years, but I'm not done griping
about *The L Word*.

LESBIAN PICKUP STRATEGIES
THAT RARELY WORK YET
ARE REPLICATED INCESSANTLY

Perfect the art of
leaning on things. Once mastered,
hook thumbs into jeans.

Drink excessively
the whole night. When she's nearby,
talk a lot louder.

Buy *Tipping the Velvet*.
Don't give it to her! Hope
she gets the "message."

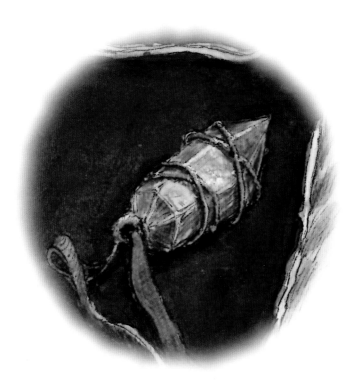

Visit a witch store.
Not for spells, just to support
local queer business!

Name obscure "shipping"
reference. When she does not
get it, run away.

Knit your feelings for
her using symbols culled from
dream dictionaries.

Say "Hi." Before she
can respond, run outside and
hail a taxi home.

Go to Trader Joe's
any day but Saturday.
(That's just good advice.)

Write a haiku book
(with cats). Fill with deep longings.
Sign hers "TRANSFERENCE."

HOW TO PICK UP . . .

The serious lesbian
Intersectional
cisgender hegemony
assimilation!

The sporty lesbian
"Is that Old Spice that
you're wearing, or . . . is that Old
Spice that you're wearing?"

The practical, cheap-cardigan-owning lesbian
"You unravel me
like H&M shirts after
two months' worth of wear."

The DIY lesbian
"My life has vastly
improved since I started to
roll my own tampons."

The lesbro
Wear Livestrong bracelet
and converse solely using
well-known *Fight Club* quotes.

The straight-looking lesbian
Say literally
anything—she's thrilled *someone*
is talking to her.

The LHB (long-haired butch)
Chat her up about
Willie Nelson and/or John
Stamos in *Full House*.

The too-cool-for-this-bar lesbian
Engage her in a
contest to see who can roll
her eyes the *hardest*.

**The deluded yet hopeful lesbian
pursuing only straight girls**
"Sexuality
is a spectrum! Let's defy
taboos with our tongues."

Your ex-girlfriend
"Snuffles and Meow-Meow
sure do miss you. Why don't you
come say hi to them?"

Your ex-girlfriend (post second breakup)
Ask her what "closure"
means to her. Then clear schedule
for at least one month.

**The grad student who maybe friend-zoned you
but you're not sure**
"I love all the bell
hooks you've been posting on your
LiveJournal account."

**The Starbucks barista whom you can't bring yourself
to make eye contact with, let alone talk to**
"I really like you
despite the fact that you serve
liquid oppression."

**The lesbian who's trying to pretend she doesn't enjoy
pop music but is dancing ecstatically**
"I've never seen a
girl dance to Taylor Swift so
ironically!"

The baby dyke
Thrust whole library
of feminist theory on
table. Walk away.

The bookish lesbian
"I wish you were the
woman sharing my bed, not
Alison Bechdel."

The SHF (short-haired femme)
"Nice [blank]!" Fill blank with
"feather," "earring," "undercut,"
or "nerdy glasses."

The hard-core bookish lesbian
Pronounce Annie Proulx's
name correctly—watch lady's
cargo pants fall off.

The obviously high lesbian
"We go together
just like peanut butter cups
and prescription drugs!"

The cat- or dog-obsessed lesbian
"You know I minored
in pet portraiture at my
women's college, right?"

The radical Marxist-feminist lesbian
"Can you believe the
phallocentric slavery
of this Bud Light Lime?"

IMAGINED AWKWARD PROPOSITIONS
FOR THE CHARACTERS YOU'RE READING
ABOUT IN YOUR BOOK CLUB

**The lesbian whom you've time-traveled back
to the Victorian Era to ask out**
Are you causing these
"uterine fits" or do I
have hysteria?

I'd be delighted
if you joined me for a ride—
you sure are hansom.

Awkward lesbian vampire proposition
You suck! I mean that
literally of course. HA-
HA. Oh, you're vegan?

Awkward lesbian werewolf proposition
I would never be
so insensitive as to
ask for doggy-style.

**Awkward lesbian velociraptor from
Jurassic Park proposition**
Hey, clever girl! What's
eating you? Me? HA-HA. Nice
claws. I dig high femme.

Awkward lesbian zombie proposition
Well, aren't you drop-
dead gorgeous? Emphasis on
Dea—[Zombie eats her.]

Awkward lesbian unicorn proposition
Has anyone told
you that you make them HORNy?
They have? Okay, great.

Awkward lesbian Bigfoot proposition
I also think that
shaving is oppressive! Do
you use rock crystals?

IMAGINED AWKWARD PROPOSITIONS
FROM FAMOUS QUEER WOMEN
THROUGHOUT HISTORY

Gertrude Stein
A lesbian is
a lesbian is a lez
who's BI-AN me drinks.

Gertrude Stein tries again
A rose is a rose
is a Rose who rose from the
bar to buy me drinks.

Gertrude Stein gets to second base
Where? *There?* You want me
to touch you there? But my dear,
there is no there there.

Billie Jean King
Love *love*! . . . Wait, come back!
It's a tennis term meaning
no one has scored. Oh.

Sappho
My muse! My favorite . . .
Aphrodite? . . . Airlea?
Ai . . . think I love you?

Georgia O'Keeffe
Here, I made you this
flower painting. It's symbolic!
Of your . . . beauty.

Audre Lorde
Eating bananas
is nice, but how about we
put them in your vag?

Susan Sontag
Sex is a pillow—
an extension of the self.
Yet suffocating.

Susan Sontag tries again
Would you like to talk
obscure French theory with
me? I hate myself.

Willa Cather
There is nothing but
the land. We are all dirt, so
shall we lie in it?

Willa Cather keeps going
I would plough you like
the godly red heaven that
is Nebraska soil.

Virginia Woolf
When I said I want
"a room of my own," I meant
"when my husband's here."

Frida Kahlo
Te adoro! Here's
a painting of me being
cruelly tortured.

DATING: IT'S NOT OK, OKCUPID

I bet many of you are wondering why this chapter exists because common knowledge has it that lesbians don't actually "date." Instead the timeline follows as such: girl meets girl, their genitals fuse together in a state of ecstatic union, and then they go raise chickens together somewhere. But that's not (always) the case! Dating and courtship are still very much a part of the lez experience. This chapter, hence, navigates the perilous waters of dating and popular websites such as OkCupid and Craigslist.

What's a "date"?
We met; we had sex;
then the next thing I knew, we
were buying wind chimes!

**To the tall, dark-haired witch from the
Moon-Worshipping Ritual**

I think you swiped my
sage stick accidentally.
I'd like it back please.

RE: To the tall, dark-haired witch from the Moon-Worshipping Ritual
I bought that sage at
Womb of One's Own, Sunray. We
need to dialogue?

RE: RE: To the tall, dark-haired witch from the Moon-Worshipping Ritual
Goddess no! But I
sure hope you purify your
soul with it, Ember.

Ahead of me at Whole Foods today
You have great taste in
nutritional yeast! I will
ignore the Craisins.

The girl in line for the Port-o-Potty with the infinity tattoo at the Canadian folk festival
I wrote a poem
about your shoulder blades. Can
I tweet it to you?

It's fated!
The way you held your
beer said Virgo. If your moon's
in Leo, call me.

**Girl in the beige multipocketed vest
working at the Berkeley REI**
I smiled at you in
my mind and never made eye
contact. You're the one.

**The woman in glasses reading Audre Lorde
at the feminist bookstore**
Let's dismantle the
master's house! Me: Plaid. Never
looked up from my book.

**Met you at the in-depth sensitivity training
for a postgender world**
By the bi . . . nary,
your views on phallocentric
highlighters moved me.

7 a.m. yoga flow class with Charity
As you were leaving,
your mat hit me in the face.
Namaste next time?

POSSIBLE FIRST MESSAGES TO WOMEN
ON ONLINE DATING SITES

I'd love it if we
could message each other for
months and never meet.

Shall we discuss our
attraction for hours and
then go home alone?

"Like being pissed on?"
an OkCupid girl asks.
"If so, urine luck."

I knew your cat's name,
diet, and hobbies before
I got to know yours.

This crush, relentless.
I am like a cat and you're
a laser pointer.

Subject: "Wanna fuck?"
Followed by "Just kidding!" Your
meaning eludes me.

Let's "Live life to the
fullest" by watching actors
on TV do it.

Her message: "I like
your socks." Tremendous! Let's build
a life together.

To the hot girls on
OkCupid: You have to
write more than "Hello . . . :)"

What the "looking for" choices really mean on OkCupid
Friends: Casual sex.
Short-term dating: Just sex. Long-
term: Face-to-face sex.

HOW TO FILL OUT YOUR DATING PROFILE LIKE A TRUE LESBIAN

Pro tip
Mastering basic
English will get you so much
ass on dating sites.

Why try online dating?
'Cause it's easier
to lie on the Internet
than to someone's face.

The first things people usually notice about me are . . .
My witchy vibe and
carefully messed-up hair or
literary tat.

That I am guiding
people in the direction
of Ultimate Truth!

I'm INTJ,
BTDUBBS! NP if U
TMI, YOLO!

That I'm riding a
star on this journey called life!
Or my undercut.

That I may still be
recovering from Saturn's
Return LOL!

HOW TO PROPOSITION
A GIRL ON FACEBOOK

How about we take
this Facebook "poking" to the
next level: book club!

Which *Titanic* scene
made you cry the hardest? "I'LL
NEVER LET GO, JACK."

I'm so attracted
to you that I'd call you on
the actual phone!

That witty Facebook
comment took me six hours. So
can we bone now please?

A SUMMARY OF ALL CRAIGSLIST
WOMEN 4 WOMEN ADS

Why is a good friend so hard to find??
The orgasm will
never be free! We must rid
it of tyranny!

No drauma!!!
Im a nice,healthy.
active,mentally girl! Please
be educated!!!!!!!!

**You: Into piercings, rectal exams,
immobilizing bondage, colonic irrigations,
enemas, nipple torture . . .**
Must also love hugs,
spooning, and *Dance Moms.* Long-term
romance possible!!!!!

Butch tenors and altos sought
Masculine women
needed to perform songs of
"classical" nature.

Where are all the real people?????
Open-minded, non-
judgmental girls only please!!!
No bisexuals.

Not looking for ms. wrong Beth Miller!!!!
No men, no couples,
no flakes, no games, no one named
Beth Miller, that whore!

RE: Not looking for ms. wrong Beth Miller!!!!
DON'T LISTEN TO MY
BITCH EX CINDY! SHE CAN'T PAY
RENT OR ATTENTION!!!!!

Don't feel blue, feel indigo!!!!
Want a "love that's true"?
Shall we "multiply life by
the Power of Two"?!?!!

Protest the inaccurate portrayal of snakes as villains and cruel beings in the media!!!
Snakes are creatures that
deserve our ssssympathy!! Join
the causssssse Augussst 3!

RE: Butch tenors and altos sought!! (REVISED)
Ad was not for sex!!!
Stop sending me pics of your
"classically trained" "flute"!!

I can't assemble this fucking IKEA bedframe
Me: Have Allen wrench,
won't travel. You: Can decode
wordless instructions.

HOW TO PROPOSITION SOMEONE WHILE
PLAYING ONLINE SCRABBLE

Play "qiviut," the
word for musk ox undercoat.
Ladies love musk ox!

'Tis better to have
loved and lost to you at Scrab—
WAIT, NO, IT ISN'T.

F U—the game I
wanna play is called Words With
Friends With Benefits.

PERFECTLY VALID EXCUSES
A LESBIAN MIGHT USE TO TURN YOU
DOWN FOR A DATE

Cosmic omens
I would date you, but
Mercury's in retrograde
until Saturday.

Harried Potter
I must finish this
paper on ontology
of Muggles' struggles.

Serious concerns
I am attending
a lecture on the social
privilege of leisure.

Ex factor
I promised my ex
that I would join her at her
birthing ritual class.

OkStupid
You thought this was a
date? "Activity partners"
are what I'm after.

Multitasking
I'm going to an
insemination ritual/
poetry reading.

Pain check!
I'd love to, but I'll
be Facebook stalking my ex
for the next nine hours.

Ex-ceptions
I promised I would
never date my ex's friends'
ex-spin instructor.

Noteworthy
I would love to but
your music collection is
not diverse enough.

The Hell Word
You identified
the most with Jenny?! I have
to leave this bar now.

A LINE OF LESBIAN-THEMED
GREETING CARDS FOR YOUR DATES

**To a person whom you have been out with several times,
though you don't know whether they were "dates"**
Thinking of you. But
mostly how you look naked.
Let's get "coffee" soon?

How about we stop
beating 'round the bush and start . . .
beating 'round the bush.

To the person who broke your really long dry spell
You please me in ways
only things with batteries
have done in the past.

To a new lover
I'll never cheat on
you with your friends 'cause I've slept
with them already.

Flirtation
I want you more than
I wanted this master's in
social work degree.

To a girl with whom you are falling in love
I look forward to
pretending to care about
your ex's chalk art.

**To a first date with whom you're not remotely
compatible but still desperately want to make out with**
Career blogging? Well,
I've heard that field is really
blowing up right now!

**To the lackluster first date whom you made out with
anyway because you couldn't face the loneliness
of existence that Thursday**
I liked you better
than I liked facing my own
crippling malaise.

**To the girl who didn't get your incredibly
obvious flirtations that 110 percent
signaled that you were into her**
Inside the card are
emojis of a peach and
dancing bunny girls.

U-HAULING

If you've been trapped under a very large boulder for the last fifty years or so, you may be unaware of the most-told lesbian joke in existence, and probably really grateful to have escaped from under that boulder! In order to help acclimate yourself back into society, you'll need to know that a lesbian brings a U-Haul to a second date because she enjoys displaying her prowess at parallel parking large trucks. And also because she's moving in with you. Lesbians love to cohabitate—Double your supply of oolong teas! Quadruple your supply of fancy mustard!—yet with this great responsibility comes an even greater cable bill. Here's how to cope with the urge to merge, the breakneck speed of a relationship's progression, and the challenge of keeping the love alive even after you've witnessed her break down over rosemary-infused crackers at Trader Joe's.

SIGNS THAT YOU'RE IN A COHABITATING
LESBIAN RELATIONSHIP

On your third date she
hands you the name of a good
couples counselor.

You can go shopping
separately and come home with
the same studded belt.

She knows where your jar
of PMS tea is and
doesn't have to ask.

Her mother sends socks
to match the pajamas she
got you for Christmas.

You spend far more time
processing the sex than you
do getting it on.

Talking at length on
identity politics
is foreplay to you.

A third of your life
is now devoted to buying
toilet paper.

You find yourself in
couples therapy six months
after breaking up.

YOU MIGHT BE IN A POLYAMOROUS
RELATIONSHIP . . .

If you answer all
questions with "Let me check my
Google Calendar."

You bring your own gloves
to the local clinic for
STI checkups.

You find that you are
flirting with someone so your
partner can bang her.

You love the way your
lover loves her other loves
but never smothers.

I scream, you scream, she
screams, we all scream! Then we all
go out for ice cream.

You do all of your
lentil and dildo shopping
in bulk at Costco.

You've had so many
orgies that three-ways start to
feel isolated.

You just didn't get
to process enough when you
were monogamous.

How a lesbian proposes
Diamonds are evil!
I found you this rock. It's how
penguins get engaged.

**A sample of lesbian wedding
and engaygement announcements**
Save the date! Our
contract with the government
includes fish tacos!

In lieu of gifts, we're
asking that guests refrain from
mocking Tofurky.

Please join Tamika
and Sally on their quest to
destroy "straight" marriage.

We don't believe in
marriage. We just really want
monogrammed towels.

A LINE OF LESBIAN-THEMED GREETING CARDS FOR YOUR LONG-TERM LOVERS

A special poem for a special lady this Valentine's Day
Roses are red, but
I don't support nonsustainable
industries.

To the überaffectionate long-term partner
I'm glad our love still
makes other people vomit
spontaneously.

Anniversary
Thank you for being
so good in bed that we can
get to sleep by nine.

There's nothing I love
more than holding you close to
avoid the wet spot.

I love you even
though your weird browsing has fucked
up my Netflix queue.

INNOVATIVE LESBIAN DATE SUGGESTIONS

Avoiding bed death in a long-term relationship can often be a struggle. The following lesbian-approved date ideas are here to help. They're crafty, cheap, and include little-known lady aphrodisiacs sure to stoke your gal's fires, and possibly convince her to donate more regularly to UNICEF. Win-win.

Have a cow (of the sea)
Attend fund-raiser
for "Conventionally
Unattractive Manatees."

Shop in a suburban outlet mall
Visit Hot Topic.
Pretend you're not *immensely*
enjoying yourself.

Furrever 21
Brainstorm names for the
all-flannel pet boutique you'd
like to one day own.

By "Let's go on a date" I meant . . .
Flipping through the Rare
Seeds catalog and eating
Kashi cereal.

Camp out in your backyard
Then renew your vows . . .
to help transient and homeless
populations!

The broke yet randy lesbian
Watch *The Craft*. Make out
each time there's a moment of
lesbian subtext.

Give me one reason to stay here
Play "How much of the
same music do we own?" Laugh/
cry accordingly.

Challenge her intellectually
Write some *Buffy the
Vampire Slayer* fan fiction—
don't be Dark Willow!

For the lesbian who craves alone time but has trouble advocating for her desires due to culturally ingrained guilt and overwillingness to please others
Organize a *hard*
scavenger hunt. While she sweats,
enjoy solitude.

Make it all about her
Let your lady pick
which documentary on
human rights to watch.

Put your love to the test
Build an IKEA
bed frame together. No one
stabbed to death? You pass.

HOW YOUR GIRL- OR BOIFRIEND
WILL PROBABLY PROPOSE

Spell out "Marry me?"
in millet on the vegan
carob muffin cake.

Buy a shelter dog.
Name it a combo of your
hyphenated names.

She asks you with a
note on your cat from your shared
Instagram account.

By replacing page
of Malm dresser instructions
with crude ring drawing.

On the back of your
Sleater-Kinney shirt, writes "Be
my Joey Ramone?"

HOW LESBIAN SEX WORKS

Lesbian sex has been confounding people since the dawn of cucumbers. What *is* it that two women do together in bed, when they're not perfecting their cross-stitch or creating nonbinary safespaces in which to embrace their intersectionality? While the Serious Lesbian will tell you, "There's no one *right* way that girls get it on, idiot," I will tell you . . . the same thing. But in a far less judgmental way. Read on to learn the ins and outs of the ol' in-and-out.

THE INS AND INS AND SOME OUTS OF LESBIAN SEX

Picture foreplay that
lasts more than a few minutes.
Now, add some crying.

Scissoring really
only appears in pornos
or in "Rock, paper . . ."

Scissoring is real!
We must take back the act from
porn. With me, Scisstors?!

Strap-on sex is fun,
until you realize you
don't know when to stop.

It's just like "porn for
women" but with less soothing
flute music playing.

It's like girl-girl porn,
but we don't compliment each
other's landing strips.

It's like porn—we can't
stop penetrating each other
with stilettos!

There's not one right way
lesbians get it on. There
are, like, four at least.

Time is built in for
improv homophone lessons
and bird metaphors.

Pour the wine, light the
fire, argue over what she
said eight months ago.

Lesbian foreplay:
Strip every time Rachel
Maddow makes a pun.

It is like straight sex,
but everyone ends up with
some hair in her mouth.

It's like straight sex, but
afterward we ask ourselves,
"We just had sex, right?"

I can't give away
the secrets but will say it
involves dream catchers.

We don't have sex; we
just pet each other until
a man comes along.

It's like straight sex, but
the little spoon is determined
by lottery.

It's like hetero
sex, but sometimes our penises
glow in the dark.

It's like straight sex, but
we don't have to rub one out
ourselves afterward.

It's like straight sex—same
regrets, insecurities—
but with more laundry.

It's like straight sex, but
by "sex," I mean deconstructing
patriarchy.

It's like straight sex, but
less worries about whether
your nipples "look weird."

Lesbian sex is
like water polo—no one
really knows the rules.

Why you should be proud
to have small hands: picking teeth,
sewing, and fisting.

Advanced techniques
It's like straight sex but
with frequent trips to Michaels
for more soy candles.

Putting the anal back in analysis
Can I Freudian
slip my finger inside your
Jung, supple body?

Who has time for sex?
We're far too busy
slowly shedding our matching
cheerleading outfits.

Options are limitless
Penises are like
boy bands: they can only move
in One Direction.

IF THE FIFTY SHADES SERIES HAD BEEN
WRITTEN BY A QUEER LADY

Fifty Shades of Spay
Protagonist finds
herself enslaved by CUTEST
tripod tabby cat.

Fifty Shades of Stay
Surprise! That "contract"
you signed was for our new time-
share in Provincetown!

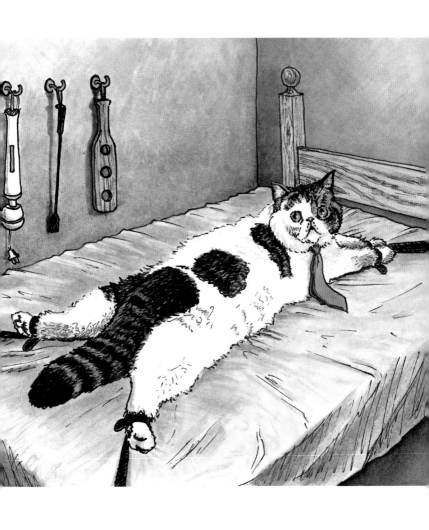

Fifty Shades of Gay
A bisexual
is born and no one questions
her identity.

Fifty Shades of Old Bay
Two industrious
gals spend all night . . . arranging
their spice cabinet.

Fifty Shades of Essay
A lesbian tome
on all that's wrong with the books.
In Papyrus font.

Fifty Shades of Bombay
In which a woman's
kink is revealed to be lip-
syncing in saris.

Fifty Shades of Tanqueray
A very drunk gal
tries to seduce a fountain
for seven hours.

Fifty Shades of A.A.
Two sober gals quickly
realize they're incompatible.
And move on.

Fifty Shades of Okay
Two women meet, and
they both respect each other's
boundaries. The End.

Fifty Shades of Bray
A lesbian tries
to explain the timeless allure
of Fran Drescher.

Fifty Shades of Sasha Grey
Lesbian admits
she has pubic hair. Her sex
life remains fine, thanks.

Fifty Shades of Buffet
Two ladies give new
meaning to the phrase "all you
can eat." Then they nap.

Fifty Shades of Sallie Mae
A forty-four-year-
old woman finally pays
off her student loans!

Fifty Shades of Crochet
Postbreakup, two girls
keep hosting the club that they
founded: Knit Happens.

Fifty Shades of Sick Pay
Pro bono lawyers
fall in love during a case
on workers' comp rights.

Fifty Shades of Papier-Mâché
A woman pretends
to be impressed by her date's
wallpaper paste art.

Fifty Shades of Hey Girl Hey
It's just like the real
books, but with Ryan Gosling,
whom lesbians love.

Fifty Shades of Hit the Hay
Two buxom beauties
learn the importance of a
good night of REM sleep.

HOW LESBIAN SEX WORKS
IN LONG-TERM COUPLES

It is our two-week
anniversary! Break out
the organic lube!

Baby, could you flip
me over? My left foot is
totally asleep.

I'm gonna rip that
grandpa sweater right offa
you when we get home.

You wanna have sex
tonight? Okay, but you have
to do all the work.

It's oddly not a
turnoff when you eat pasta
out of the strainer.

The sweatpants from Old
Navy manage to stay on
the entire time.

It's midnight! If you
wanted a piece of this, you
should have asked at ten.

But I just washed the
sheets! Okay, fine, I'll arrange
towels artfully.

Three times in one week!
My, it's just like we're twenty-
one years old again!

Let's wait till after
Orange Is the New Black. No,
the next episode.

Nibbling her makes you
realize you're hungry, so
you stop for waffles.

Mmm, I can't wait to
sit on your face for, like, five
minutes 'cause my knees.

She whips out restraints.
You shiver with delight, say:
"Wait, let me pee first."

You might not want to
go downtown tonight—there's a
southern wind blowin'.

I would love to fuck
you senseless . . . but I just ate
all that saag paneer.

That's right, baby, right
there, get that tax refund, don't
stop, get it, get it.

Someone has to clean
off the clothes on the bed first.
No? Then tomorrow.

For the love of all
that's sacred: It's called foreplay.
Think outside my box!

The G-spot is like
mercantilism. I know
it exists. That's it.

It's like straight sex, but
you aren't labeled a slut for
fucking on first dates.

It's like straight sex but
with more slouchy blazers and
P!nk dance remixes.

When lesbians say
"all night long," they do not mean
forty-five minutes.

"What do two girls do
together in bed, really?"
Two words: gin rummy.

On nights out/anniversaries/romantic holidays
Sex occurs before
you go out 'cause you know you'll
be too tired after.

A word of caution
Hitachi Magic
Wands have two settings: "low" and
"immersion blender."

It's like straight sex but
with more IKEA wardrobe
storage assemblage.

It's like straight sex, but
first we have to consult our
lunar calendars.

On the prevalence of dental dams
Ha ha ha ha ha
ha ha ha ha ha ha ha
ha . . . ha ha ha ha.

Dental dams reprise
They'd get more use if
they had a more appealing
name, like beaver dams.

Working out the kinks
Jameson shots and
standard police handcuffs do
not mix. Lesson learned.

How lesbians discuss porn
Of course, I loved Crash
Pad's "Fisting: Lend a Hand," but
the book was better.

GROUP SEX:
THE MORE THE HAIRIER

A true story
At the lez orgy,
the biggest bed contained two
women JUST spooning.

Sex party rules of conduct
Consent, consent, and
please bring a baked good to share
with everyone.

Sex party rules continued: hot tub etiquette
What makes us soooo wet?
Radical self-reliance
on your own towel!

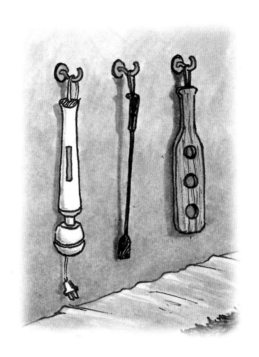

Whip it good
What a spirited
flogging! Maybe next time no
GMO lecture?

Pleather is better
Who wants to get fucked?
My toys accommodate all
types of allergies!

SEX THROUGH THE AGES

Sex in your teens
After a *Buffy*
viewing: "You're not going to
tell your boyfriend, right?"

Shhh, we have to be
very quiet so that my
parents don't hear us!

Sex in your twenties
I'm pretty sure it
was good, but that may have just
been the tequila.

It's like duck, duck, goose,
but the ducks are all your friends
and so is the goose.

Elevators, Gap
dressing rooms, coat closets—all
locales are fair game.

Sex in your thirties
We can open this
second bottle of wine or
have sex. But not both.

Mmm, baby, yes, oh,
not so loud, baby, you will
wake the baby, oh!

A *hotel* bed? I
didn't know we were getting
kinky over here!

"Can your parents hear
us?" "Who cares! We've been married
for several years!"

Sex in your forties
Quick, the kids are out,
so I've readied the *Bareback
Mountain* DVD.

You are not above
bartering sex favors to
not do the dishes.

Sex in your fifties
Let's do that role-play
scene where I get to lie on
my back the whole time.

You menopausal?
'Cause, girl, you put the hot back
into hot flashes.

Sex in your sixties
You find that you are
suddenly concerned about
STIs again.

Sex in your seventies
I should tell you that
I'm bi . . . onic. And this hip
is titanium.

Sex in your eighties
Fuck me until I
can't remember my name! Wait,
what is it again?

DOS AND DON'TS

Trimmed nails are a MUST.
Trimmed everything else is
always a surprise.

A surefire way to drive the ladies wild
Well-manicured hands
have the effect muscled abs
have on straight women.

Approved lesbian dirty talk
I don't care if it
takes hours, tell me about your
doctoral thesis.

Part those lips for a
slice of gluten-free, cheese-free,
conflict-free "pizza."

This drum circle is
so primal. Don't you feel at
one with Mother Earth?

Shall we deconstruct
dominant signifiers
over wine tonight?

I got you a Green
Party bumper sticker to
match your Subaru.

Guess what? I received
a National Endowment
for the Arts stipend!

Want to deconstruct
hegemonic power structures?
That's what SHE said.

Things you should never say after sex
Next let's try reverse-
cowgirl scissor from *Blue Is
the Warmest Color.*

That was fantastic!
Nice use of scuba gear. Did
it sound like I came?

I cannot wait to
edit this footage and put
it on Instagram!

If I were reading
this wet spot like tea leaves, I'd
say: Call your mother.

Well, that was as
uninspiring as my tarot
cards predicted.

Now I get why your
ex said it was just like a
hospital sponge bath!

"Is this Tegan and
Sara? That was *our* song." (Sobs.)
"Which one?" "All of them!"

What to say to all women after sex
You must be famished!
Let's wear loose pants and raid the
fridge like we are bears.

Note that many of these premises are based on actual scenes in real porn films.

**A precocious young lass has something to share
with her Catholic schoolgirl classmates**
A zine with Ani
lyrics, *Glee* fan fiction, and
the merits of plaid.

**Two blondes engage in some
much-sought-after pussy play**
Susan and Chris knew
how understaffed the local
no-kill shelter was.

**Horny amateur babe wearing pajamas her mother
bought her at Lands' End loves dirty-talking her lover
(a Ph.D. candidate in musicology)**
"I want to make sweet
consensual love to this
nondairy ice cream."

Cohabitating co-eds in lust swap many secrets
"Take off your shirt," she
commands. "This soap I made has
no skin irritants."

A busty babe's first time kissing her flatmate
Ten hot seconds, and
then ten months of "What did it
mean?" conversations.

Naughty lesbian babysitter has a surprise
for Dad when he returns home
She let the kids stay
up until eleven to
watch *Harry Potter*.

Hot MILFs engage in a steamy clam photo sesh
One arranges bread
while the other gets the best
Instagram angle.

Bicurious girls want to experiment
May expects Beck to
make a move. Beck thinks May will.
They die celibate.

**Big-boobed sorority sisters satisfy
each other's every desire**
Tofutti Cuties,
Hulu, and analyzing
Liz Phair videos.

**Petite redhead and *caliente* Latina roommates
surprise the pizza delivery man . . .**
With a lecture on
how his boss should compost all
used pizza boxes.

IF LESBIANS WERE IN CHARGE OF
DEFINING COMMON SEX POSITIONS

Reverse cowgirl
Reverse gender
outlaw in a typically male-
dominated field

Missionary
"Proselytizing
of global, indigenous
people" position

Doggy-style
"A four-legged soul
mate whose nurturance and depth
exceeds humans'" style

Blow job
Blow "We demand pay
equity, plus some decent
maternity leave"

The spoon
The "Why don't you look
me in the eye while making
love anymore, Anne?"

Tea-bagging
Organic, bio-
available, sustainable
balls in your face

The wheelbarrow
Migrant farmworkers
have deplorable working
conditions—sign this!

The rocket
The "We resent this
phallocentric metaphor.
Please change to 'love cave.'"

Woman on top
No changes required.
—Fondly, every lesbian
in the entire world

The spin cycle (a.k.a. sex on a washing machine)
This is not what we
meant by more equal household
chore distribution.

LOOK BOTH WAYS: DEMYSTIFYING BISEXUALITY

You've probably heard a lot of stereotypes and jokes about bisexuality, a.k.a. the redheaded goth stepchild of sexual orientations. Most people can't even agree on a definition of bisexuality, which has led to a lot of confusion, angst, and reality shows starring Tila Tequila.

Ironically, part of the reason bisexuality gets a bad rap—and why so few people openly identify as such—is because it's associated with so many negative cultural connotations. For our purposes, I'll define a bisexual as someone who is drawn to emotional and/or sexual relationships with different genders, although terms relating to bisexuality run the gamut and can include descriptors such as "pansexual," "queer," "ambisexual," "omnisexual," "fluid," and "Larry King." Below are the truest and most definitive haiku that document the sexual identity that is often shrugged off as a "phase," a "gateway," "homosexuality lite," or "Fifty Shades of Gay."

WHAT'S A BISEXUAL?

According to douche canoes
Only the bread to
my favorite sandwich, bro!
Amirite? Up top!

According to scientists who study bisexuality
It's the only way
I know to get paid to watch
gay porn all day long.

According to your conservative mom
Why must you punish
me? Was it because I wore
so many pantsuits?

According to your liberal hippie mom
Love is love! I had
spiritual intercourse
with a redwood once.

According to *National Geographic*
As documented
by ten thousand species of
animals: Thursday.

According to Tom Cruise
Thursday. Or as it's
permitted by Xenu, the
Galactic Mogul.

**According to beersexuals, a.k.a. girls
who make out with girls solely to turn guys on**
Three parts vodka and
two parts "It seemed so fun in
Katy Perry's song!"

**According to the guys who benefit from
beersexuals' exhibitionism**
WHOO-OO-OOO-OO-OOOO
OO-OO-OO-OO-WHOO-OO-OO
OO-OOO-O-OO-OO!

According to unicorns
IT'S THOSE BITCHES WHO
STOLE OUR NAME. NOW WE ARE FORCED
TO GO BY STEVE. *STEVE!*

According to "family values" Republicans
A HORROR SHAME PLAGUE.
(Unless the act takes place in
an airport bathroom.)

HOW DOES BISEXUAL SEX WORK?

It's like straight sex, but
you still get to imagine
Portia de Rossi.

It's like straight sex, but
there are more people to high-
five when you're finished.

It's like the "Mindful
Raccoon" in acro yoga,
but less crotch grabbing.

It's like gay sex but
with infinitely more puns
involved. Come again?

Pro: There are a lot
of choices! And con: There are
a lot of choices!

Fine. It's like straight sex.
Get off our backs already,
and get on our backs!

It's like straight sex, but
your sheets will be covered in
glitter eye makeup.

It's like straight sex, but
less ambient techno and
more David Bowie.

It's like gay sex but
with more trivia about
the bonobo ape.

It's like gay sex, but
brunch counts as foreplay. IF IT
DOESN'T, THEN IT SHOULD.

COMMON BISEXUAL QUESTIONS POSED TO NONBISEXUAL PEOPLE

Straight people exist?
I read otherwise in a
New York Times think piece.

So, you're gay, huh? Do
you make out with boys just to
turn men on, or what?

You like brunettes AND
redheads? You straights can never
make up your damn minds.

Hetero? Is that
why you have so much trouble
with monogamy?

Are you sure? I think
you probably just haven't
met the right man yet?

Threesome? Sandwich? Three-
way? Ménage à trois? Group sex?
3P? Screwnicorn?

Monosexual?
I guess I respect your choice
to limit yourself.

BREAKING UP
IS HARD TO DO

Breaking up is hard to do for anyone, but for gaydies, it's nearly impossible. Somewhere, at this very moment, a lesbian couple has been trying to break up for the last several decades. By the time you finish this intro, they'll have made up yet again, having moved on to the cry-cuddle phase of lesbian reconciliation (more on that below). No one is really sure why lesbians need to end relationships multiple times before it sticks, and a few more times after that before they can cook lentils together without it ending in sloppy, soupy rebound sex and a lot of unnecessary laundry. To lesbians, a breakup is like a sub club card—except when you get to ten, you're rewarded not with a delicious sandwich but with six months of postbreakup couples therapy. The following haiku will deal with the right and wrong way to handle a breakup (excuse me, "relationship transition"), school you in the fine art of "letting girls down," and explain the dual nature of rebounds (a.k.a. "meeting your next monogamous partner").

A REPRESENTATIVE SAMPLE OF EVERY LESBIAN BREAKUP THROUGHOUT HISTORY IN TWELVE WORDS

I can't date you, but
here's an ambiguous poem
about my feelings.

HOW TO BREAK UP WITH A LESBIAN

It can't be done. You're
welcome to try again next
year, if you insist.

Tell her that you loved
the Star Wars prequels more than
the originals.

Set aside tissue
boxes, and the next thirty-
four years of your life.

Wars are fought over
who gets to keep the tribal
pantsuit in the split.

It's been six months. You
finally feel close to defining
your "boundaries."

Been single four months
now. Ate croutons for dinner.
There's no connection.

I can't date you, but
here's a Spotify playlist
about how I feel.

She has a new girl,
a house, stability. I
have Facebook comments.

A LINE OF LESBIAN-THEMED GREETING CARDS FOR EXES

To the ex who defriended you on Facebook because you disagreed about the dimensionality of the female characters in *The Great Gatsby*
I forgive you for
being wrong about everything
(and dumping me).

To your ex whom you're still sleeping with
"Processing" with you
is my favorite kind of
aerobic workout.

To the ex you haven't seen in a long time but still entertain thoughts of sleeping with
I'd love to get back
in touch. Specifically
with your genitals.

To the ex you'll soon date again
This time I mean it!
It's over. We're through. What are
you doing Thursday?

HOW TO LET A QUEER GIRL
DOWN GENTLY

I would invite you
up, but I still share a bed
with my ex-girlfriend.

I must tend to my
succulents, flying squirrel,
and hemp marinade.

I can't date you, but
here's how you can degrease your
hair with raw cacao.

Past-life regression
coach says that I'm not ready
to date in this life.

I said I'd perform
long-distance Reiki on my
ex-girlfriend's sick cat.

HOW TO PISS OFF AN EX INDEFINITELY

It pains me to say
it, but your mother was right
about you, sorry.

THE WRONG WAY TO GRIEVE A BREAKUP

Clutching this forty
like it was you in my arms . . .
was going too far.

Seriously might
consider adding Facebook
"pokes" to my number.

I love you, I love
you, I love you. Seriously,
though, don't call me.

HOW TO BREAK UP WITH FICTIONAL CHARACTERS WHO WERE IMPLICITLY OR EXPLICITLY LESBIANS

Beaker the Muppet
"You're a little too
selfish. It's always about
meeee-meeee-meeee-meeee-meee."

Shane from *The L Word*
On the surface, be
a "cool mom." Then, light her skate
shop on fire. Burn!

Peppermint Patty from *Peanuts*
Repeatedly ask
"Why are there so many balls?"
while watching softball.

How Sherlock Holmes refuses to let Watson break up with him
"Give it up, old chap!
You have been trying since
1887."

Fluttershy from *My Little Pony*
"Darling Fluttershy,
while our friendship is magic,
our sex life is not."

THE TWELVE STAGES OF LESBIAN BREAKUP GRIEF

Denial
Mid-breakup-process,
engage in "breakup sex" while
you are both crying.

Cat adoption
You've always wanted
pets named after prominent
artistic dykons!

Anger
Throw out your shared sex
toys. Don't even recycle
them! She's not worth it.

Revenge
Compost her beloved
organic herb garden. Thyme's
on *whose* side now, bitch?

Sadness
Imagine which cat
will probably eat you first
when you die alone.

Guilt about not recycling sex toys
Remove the sex toys
from the trash. Mother Earth thanks
you—if not that tramp!

Return adopted cats
Vow to come back for
Gertrude and Alice once you're
"in a better place."

Requisite posting of Craigslist hookup ad
"Looking for no-strings-
attached fun! Let's bone and then
never speak again!"

Meet Craigslist hookup from ad
Once attraction is
established, talk for hours,
plan *Glee* marathon.

**Date Craigslist hookup exclusively
for the next one to two years**
She's not someone you
really see dating "long term,"
but she has great hair.

**Break up with Craigslist hookup
turned monogamous girlfriend**
Make up seventeen
minutes later. Wonder, "Does
anyone *get* me?"

**Break up with Craigslist hookup
turned monogamous girlfriend again**
If it sticks, congrats!
Return to the first stage of
Lesbian Breakups.

REBOUNDS

Rebounded with my
ex while watching *Bound*. Now we're
bound for therapy.

Does it count as a
rebound if it is with the
woman who dumped you?

The moment when you
realize your rebound has
dated your ex too.

Change your dildo's name
to Obama. Have the
audacity to hope.

Have debates over
whether to use Obama
with new girls you meet.

When debate stalemates,
take Obama out. What a
solid listener.

In prayers, you ask
God why aren't there a few
more gaydies on earth?

"Listen," He replies.
"I've got my hands full right now
with Kristen Stewart."

You stop praying and
rebounding with your dildo.
Back to therapy.

MY EX IS YOUR EX: THE UPS AND DOWNS OF BEING LOVERS AND FRIENDS AND EXES

Remember when Jay-Z wrote in his song—appropriately titled "99 Problems"—that he had "ninety-nine problems but a bitch ain't one"? Well, as I mentioned earlier, lesbians have ninety-nine problems and ninety-eight of them are "bitches." (The ninety-ninth problem is reconciling the rampant misogyny in rap lyrics with their super catchy beats.) This chapter will deal with common lesbian problems, such as the fact that 85 percent of us have the same haircut, how frequently we date our friends' exes (it's not a dating pool; it's a dating puddle), how to differentiate a lesbian from a garden-variety hipster, and what to do if you are sleeping with a carbon copy of yourself.

SERIOUS, INSURMOUNTABLE LESBIAN PROBLEMS

A wheel good time
Some days, it seems the
only appreciation
comes from men in cars.

Netfux
We will endure the
crappiest movies to see
two minutes of GAY.

Double your pleasure
Two periods, two
wet spots, and EIGHT HUNDRED TRACY
CHAPMAN ALBUMS.

Great ex-pectations
You are forever
waiting for the toaster that
you have been promised.

The difficult art of flirtation
To the wrong women:
you're predatory. The right
ones: you're TOO SUBTLE.

Fashion
People tell you that
you dress like you're a '90s
movie cameo.

Fashion, take two
You definitely
need to have that many beanies
in your wardrobe.

You look familiar
It's like straight sex, but
replace "one"-night stand with "one
hundred and fourteen."

Intrusive family members
No one ever says
that "you just haven't met the
right ham sandwich yet!"

Your makeout music is the same music that plays when . . .
People die on *Grey's Anatomy*, thus killing all lady boners.

From the lesbian committee on political correctness
We request that "big spoon" be replaced with "body-actualized spoon."

When explaining to your parents why you insist on working for nonprofits
"I've decided to stay on another year." "So you hate money then?"

From the lesbian committee on political correctness, again
We request that you never Facebook "poke" someone without her consent.

How lesbian sexting works
Autocorrect turns
"mmm" to "mom." Freud rises from
grave: "I told you so!"

On making long-distance work
Skype sex? Can't you just
masturbate to my Facebook
pics like usual?

Only straight girls seem to flirt with you
I'm used to women
that I date being straight, but
never straightforward.

People accuse you of narcissism
I'm fucking someone
who looks just like me. It's my
own doppelbanger.

A concerned email from my ex
It's been four years since
you left and I'm STILL dating
people you dated.

You look doubly familiar
My fuck buddies are
now fucking each other and
not me. Fucking great.

A lesbian greeting card for the distant family member
who says homophobic things during the holidays
"Congrats! You're a
monster." (But written in glitter
so it feels festive!)

HIPSTER APPROPRIATION OF LESBIAN CULTURE: A MANIFESTO IN FIVE HAIKU

First they came for our
small-batch pickled kohlrabi,
and we said nothing.

Then they came for our
plaid, and we blogged a little
but still said nothing.

Then they came for our
light beer, and we tweeted passive-
aggressively.

Then they came for our
mullets, and . . . we let that one
slide, actually.

Then they came to our
bars and WE HIT ON ALL OF
THEM BY ACCIDENT!

A common stereotype among partnered queer ladies is the dreaded "lesbian bed death"—that is, the notion that queer ladies stop getting it on once they've merged. While I believe this is an "affliction" that happens to all couples in long-term relationships, and should hence be called "NO, *YOU* HAVE BED DEATH," I will grant the notion that perhaps lesbians are too busy saving things—whales, rain forests, Jennifer Beals's career—to focus on sex for any consistent amount of time. There are ways to avoid bed death, however. One example, as my ex-girlfriend pointed out, is to not refer to your partner's vagina as "God's refrigerator." Below is a list for how to avoid bed death and keep the love alive!

Serve her breakfast in
bed. Tell her it's not 'cause you
don't own a table.

Leave a trail of rose
petals leading to her futon
mattress on the floor.

When your girlfriend's ex
shows up at brunch, counsel her
with Etsy advice.

Take her out to fancy restaurants
"My love for you is
as limitless as breadsticks
at Olive Garden."

COMMON REASONS A LESBIAN MAY SUDDENLY AND INEXPLICABLY CRY

A lesbian alone already has a WORLD OF FEELS. Add another lesbian into the mix and you've got the makings of every Mariah Carey song in existence. Or a lot of crying. Which is fine! Ritual face-wetting is healthy for us, probably. I don't know, I'm not a doctor. If I were, it'd be weird that I was writing this book. Unless I lost a dare or something. In which case it would prove I either had really amazing friends or that my friends were assholes. Thank God I don't have to think about situations like this, is what I'm saying! Otherwise I might cry. Also, the following are a few reasons you or your lady might find yourselves weeping.

The first-blush-of-love cry
It's just amazing
how much she *gets you* after
only two short dates!

The first-blush-of-doubt cry
Ugh, it's been two dates
and it's like she doesn't get
your essence *at all*!

The cry-because-she's-crying cry
You feel sad because
she feels sad because: war, strife,
poverty, and Crocs.

The circular-reasoning cry
You feel sad because
she feels sad 'cause she's afraid
of making you sad!

The cry because the sex is so good and it's been so long
And also because
Adele is playing. Why did
she put Adele on?

**The cry because the sex is
rather painful actually but you don't want to
hurt her feelings and make her cry too**
She fucked me so hard
it's like she was looking for
my virginity!

The drunken cry
Youuuu! You's more perfect
than a Tegan and Sara
song! You superstaah!

The unpleasant-astrological-prediction cry
Our birth charts aren't
compatible! Your Ruler's
Mars and mine's Venus!

The laugh-cry
"Bet last night was fun,"
said your boss while pointing at
the lube in your bangs.

A LINE OF LESBIAN-THEMED GREETING CARDS FOR YOUR FRIENDS

Thanks for being a
friend in my time of need. And
by "friend," I mean slut.

It's redundant to
say you're gay *and* that you majored
in theater tech.

What a hot night! I'm
so glad you figured out you're
actually straight.

PERFECTLY LEGITIMATE REASONS WHY A LESBIAN MIGHT SLEEP WITH HER FRIENDS

Plenty of fish in
the sea! And plenty of
Smirnoff in this bottle.

We take the concept
of recycling VERY
SERIOUSLY.

How else could you get
access to the premium
cable channels, huh?

You wanted to spend
time with her cat, but ended
up with her pussy.

To prove the last girl
wrong. MY FIGURE EIGHT TECHNIQUE
IS SOLID, NICOLE.

Because her bed has
a legit mattress, with a
frame and everything!

So you'd have fodder
for an empowering folk
song or a haiku.

The brief walk home was
TOO FAR and it was below
seventy degrees!

I don't want to be
in a relationship! Just
with you constantly.

Because it was a
particularly moving
Roseanne episode.

THE PERKS OF BEING FRIENDS WITH A LESBIAN

Would never, ever
shame you for knowing the theme
song to *Dawson's Creek*.

Thrilled to lend you a
cowboy hat or bolo tie
for costume parties.

Will tell you that your
'90s fashion sense never
will go out of style.

Always have access
to nail clippers, no matter
the circumstances.

We will always ask
what you are thinking—many,
many times a day!

Clown school? Septum ring?
A third Ph.D.? All great
and wise life choices.

ACKNOWLEDGMENTS

FROM ANNA

This book would not have been possible without the tireless efforts, input, and inspiration from my girlfriend, Kelsey Beyer. Without your crazy-genius talent, compassion, and support, I would be so lost. Thank you. And to my family: Theresa and Bob Geary, John Pulley, and Jonny Pulley. I'm incredibly lucky to call you kin.

Big, big ups also go to Mac McClelland for her help in getting this book off the ground and for being my self-esteem cheerleader and role model. Thanks to Bob Miller and Jasmine Faustino at Flatiron Books for being so amazing. Thanks to Alexis Coe for believing in all my weird little projects, and to the fine folks at *The Toast*—Nicole Cliffe, Mallory Ortberg, and Nikki Callahan—for publishing some of these haiku and letting me write poems about Tegan's and Sara's bone structure. To Ammie Brod, my unofficial editor of everything, you are indispensable and a damn joy of a human being. Thanks to Ellie (squish!) and Devon (*ma petite chou-fleur*) for making life interesting.

To Kelly Underman, Marie McIntosh, Katherine Harte DeCoux, Allison Moon, Ellen Martel, Tristan Crane, and my Facebook and Twitter friends who contributed haiku inspiration and ideas. And of course, to all the gals who rejected me. Without you, this book would have been much shorter.

FROM KELSEY

Thanks to my parents, Molly and Bill, and my brother, Dannel, for all their undying support (and for putting up with my neuroses) over the years. And of course to Anna, without whom I may never have had the opportunity to illustrate a book of lesbian sex haiku with suggestive cat drawings, and who makes me laugh and inspires me every day.

I would also like to thank Fallon Young for her shockingly successful efforts as a matchmaker, for always supporting my work, and for inspiring me to draw my first lesbian cats. And Toni Sicola and Gillian Fitzhugh for educating me on many of the finer points of "Lesbian 101" in my early twenties, without which I would most likely understand far fewer of the references in this book. And my dear friend Robin Weinert, for always sharing his critical eye and telling me in no uncertain terms when something is fucking done.

Many thanks to Maru for his role in inspiring the concept of this book and all his groundbreaking work with boxes over the years, to Tony Danza (may he rest in peace), Franklin, Bella, Snugglecat, Door, Gray Kitty, and all the anonymous cats who made this book possible. Also to Rachel Wilson, Hannah Chastain, Claire Taylor, Liz and Kate, and all my exes and friends who sent me pictures and gave me feedback and inspiration. And to my therapist, obviously.

ABOUT THE AUTHOR
AND THE ILLUSTRATOR

ANNA PULLEY is a writer in Oakland, California. Her work has appeared in *New York* magazine and *Mother Jones,* on BuzzFeed, AlterNet, The Toast, and Salon, and in zines tastefully peppered with Ani DiFranco lyrics. She's been a repeat guest on Dan Savage's podcast, *Savage Love,* and is a sex and relationship columnist for the *Chicago Tribune* and AfterEllen. Visit annapulley.com or let her send you overly personal e-mails at tinyletter.com/annapulley.

KELSEY BEYER is an artist living in Oakland. She specializes in prints, drawings, illustrations, and figure modeling. Her work has been featured on Foulmouth Greetings cards, in the National Queer Arts Festival, on The Toast, and in *Gay Men Draw Vaginas.* She has been moonlighting as the unofficial visual documentarian for the Bay Area's favorite girl orgy since 2009. See more of her work at kelseybeyer.com.

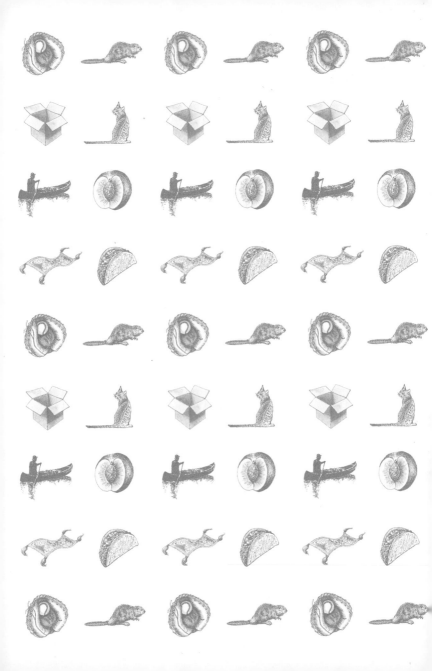